THE ROSE CONCORDANCE

THE ROSE CONCORdANCE

ANGELA CARR

BookThug | Toronto | *MMIX*

The production of this book was made possible through the generous assistance of The Canada Council for The Arts and the Ontario Arts Council.

 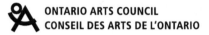

Printed in Canada.

LIBRARY AND ARCHIVES CANADA CATALOGUING IN PUBLICATION

Carr, Angela, 1976-
    The rose concordance / Angela Carr.

Poems.
ISBN 978-1-897388-46-4

    I. Title.

PS8605.A773R68 2009   c811'.6   C2009-904681-4

"For although this mirror world may have many aspects, indeed infinitely many, it remains ambiguous, double-edged. It blinks: it is always this one – and never nothing – out of which another immediately arises."

Walter Benjamin, *The Arcades Project*

"Mon cuer seul por quoi i envoi?"

Guillaume de Lorris, *Le roman de la rose*

THE ROSE CONCORDANCE

CONCOR*d*ANCE-CORRIDORS

OF FOUNTAINS
AND VANITIES

of the font to the fountain no avail

of the font to the fountain no avail

of the font to the fountain no avail

of the font to the fountain no avail

of the font to the fountain no avail

of the font to the fountain no avail

of the font to the fountain no avail

of the font to left haunting no avail

of the font to left haunting no avail

of the font to the fountain no avail

of the font to the fountain no avail
of the font to the fountain no avail
of the font to the fountain no avail

of/fo untain

come puiz ou come fountain
eating light or eating fountain
come une fontaine soz une pine
soz le pin la fontaine assise
under a pin this fountain satisfies
soz le pin clear and sane
when il vint à la fontaine
qu'il musa à la fontaine

of alarm and fountains

that i isolated and romanced this fountain
reading in the nakedness of self-contained spray
such diffuse words
how i love words
if this word is a hood
episodically thrust downward to reveal "fountains"
i recovered
the fountain is a hood
soft material fountaining
i obsessed over its advantage
i understood fashion anew
as one single movement into depths of earth
sex's humectant randomness alarmed me
i mirrored the rhetoric of employment
in this tactical handshake
we are "friends"
the sparkling stones of the fountain have scraped my palms

of critical and naive confusion

let's say that in this presocial fountain we splash freely
i'd like to naively delete the deiform source
in this critically naive and
complicitous gamble with humanism
of the prefeminist fountain, gushing is essential
existence is an aromatic crease
credulous and rich secretions
and now in my hands an encyclopaedic gathering
such confusions
such praise as circulates in critically fleshy fountains
inferentially junked theologies in a pile on the floor
inferentially junked theologies collecting attributes on the floor
choosing abjection is a stance of defiance?
is this the critical substance of drank?
your art given as fleshy keepsake?

of the attribute

fashion wants to discover essential attributes
its movement like archaeology
i said one direct motion downward
no you said that's drilling
would you develop this metaphor, comparing archaeological
sites with oil rigs?
my interest is in accidental attributes
neither to abuse accidentally nor to mesmerize
when i take off my gloves in spring
when i write to her in vain
and the vanity of cities

of fountains and vanities

fading out the fountain
vanities saved on film
i factured an urban garden on the film's fringes
now there are american hedges vainly bordering
i heave music, its whole beautiful category, vainly
through the film
several twigs snap off the hedge
picaresque music saddens vanity
strangely enough vanity weeps in the fountain
did you think the fountain wept?
vainly wishing it were sacrosanct
vanity weeps on the edge of strangeness
vanity blurs the edge but by no means obliterates it
similitude of vanity and fountain
blue criss-crossings in the fountain

of the fountain it is the end

of the fountain hurries me

of the fountain clear and sane

of the fountain would have been fountains

of the fountain under the pine

of the fountain seated under the pine

of the fountain hurries me

of the fountain it is the end

of the fountain reflects me

of the fountain is flesh

of the fountain through love

of the fountain if you come

SLEEP WATER

"Standing small and insubordinate, he would watch the
basins of the fountain loosing their skirts of water in
a ragged and flowing hem, sometimes crying to a
man's departing shadow, "Aren't you the beauty!"
                                    Djuna Barnes, *La Somnambule*

A somnambulist rests in the sunlight in this antique postcard
Touched up with maverick colours   Mauve emerging in a
reclining sky like
                    an ache emerging in the authentic, splitting it

His shoes are beside the fountain's basin and he is behind the
perimeter of trees   Elsewhere   He is at the edge of vanishing
behind faded trees   clouds of green paint superseding them
How like the present   How colour in the postcard approaches
authentic colour

20

The anarchy of the fountain is an absence of water   Instead buffeting violet light on the downward arc from a splendidly perched upper basin

The upper basin is important, not unlike colour, to any notion of the authentic   The upper basin is intrinsic yet supplemental, a bird's perch, an unattainable accessory both toweringly majestic and superfluous like a figure head whose style is a belated container   a raised basin for grey areas

In the absence of colour the coolness of his palm cupping his cheek   Where he is just beyond the perimeter of trees   Parallel shadows of vanishing trees

Nevertheless a confusion of styles   The ghosting and fading style engaging a felicitous anarchy in which authenticity could be a horizontal fountain if we were even to consider authenticity a perimeter

Colours culminate in a raised basin for grey areas

The monism of a splendidly perched upper basin evokes the venues in which we read this poetry aloud   Our mouths before the microphones   Bodies paralleling images of tall and slender fountains   How superfluous is the authority of our speaking voices   How superfluous our height   There is the appearance of water all around us   Like the torn and floating pages of books

The anarchy of this poetry is like the colour of leaves, tending imprecisely toward the authentic   The anarchy of this poety is an absence of books   Instead buffeting violet light on the downward arc from a splendidly perched upper basin

Few books are read by him and even fewer read from cover to cover

Cartilage of the reader, the book's completion is a softness

The somnambulist dwells in motion In the dalliance of light on the fountain   There is the appearance of water all around

CONCORDANCES

à retraduire: de couleur

retouchée de couleurs sauvages fauves
tellement la couleur dans l'image de
tend vers la couleur authentique
importante, comme la couleur, pour toute
en l'absence de couleur la fraîcheur
les couleurs culminent en un bassin
comme la couleur une absence

of the authentic

authentic fissure
authenti cfissure
authent icfissure
authen ticfissure
authe nticfissure
auth enticfissure
aut henticfissure
au thenticfissure

OF THE PRECIOUS

of the precious

to have a precious lover
a precious kindness
what i could not promise
of these hundred precious books
take what's mine and precious
now subterfuge and blue
doubts sweep a bare and
precious backdrop
don't wait for me to choose
preciously between
meaning and coincidence

preciously the covers
and the stones of blue ink
are transformed presently
the shhhhhh of soft
and contrary kisses/

and sighs of worse preciousness
of these hundred precious books
do they suspect wrongly?
in whose night and day were types of grain argued
most passionately?
in luxury's garden
asleep as though
my precious eyes
i cannot see her

of the worst

this felony is worsening
a hundred pairs of worse ch
irrs chastity you worsen me
worch comes in my bed
and softens the worst of th
worst bitterness is a wet mouth
i read this worst love is a no

worsening and other eyelets
in bed my aunt wakes me with toast
nakedness of a delicious word convenience

of running, of the core

how running dryly from complicity

running dryly with fragile limbs

nothing runs more beautifully than instinct

no one runs more beautifully

to poverty when running yields

runners, these aspects, leaves in her hair.

can you fashion such a beautiful runner?

my heart races

it appears softly enough

presumably slows your running

the running of our voices changes nothing

how the smell runs into me

running and the smell of your body

i say running when i mean to say bodies

the bodies of our voices change nothing

how bodies dryly from complicity

bodies dryly with fragile limbs

nothing bodies more beautifully than instinct

no one bodies more beautifully

poverty for whom bodies cede

bodies, these aspects, leaves in her hair.

can you fashion such a beautiful body?

my heart races

it appears softly enough

presumably slows your body

the bodies of our voices change nothing

how the smell embodies me

bodies and the smell of you running

i say bodies when i mean to say running

the running of our voices changes nothing

of confusion and covers

if our love has been outdistanced
confusion of claustrophobia and breaking waves
of vast blueness and covers
in this confused complement
tending a floral flush
where wine decompresses
and sumptuous difference quivers
confused i copy her handwriting
under hers (luxury's)
cover

just when i said
mine is inner confusion
i would be forever separate from her
discovering conversation
heaped handfuls
morning leaves tenderly confused

nostalgia is dew
covers a surrender
to the logic of vocations
where residual confusion

of covers and of seeming

covers dance and note
engulfed in huge coverings
of satiety and satisfaction
uncover the manuscript
where laughter seems welcome
her hand covered in pine needles
what uncovered loves?
when the poem covers bitterness
almond blossoms are plentiful
seemingly she writes to me
it seems there should be quotes here

monogamous love are you in pain?
over love runs the tail of mutton
outrageous and maligned covers
will you cover me then?

from the pasture where you sing sweetly

what long nights and days the covers languished
who has no power to cover
who slips under the cover of a heart
who got under the covering and wrote

of nearness

that i dare near him to speak volubly
now a tertiary nearness i must leave
envy oh those near leaving
me now near the vanishing
(as if never near a smaller thing)
little by little if i interject
this button of yes-nearly-loving
(and know that i am nearly)
bears remaining's weight
a wetness nearly adjusting
know well, when i flee nearby
if nearness that soft button feels
i will nearly return
trampling tender grasses

of the courier

forbidden access to the fountain
at night coursing furtively
fortuitously splashing another pair
bright coursings of sex is
a misleading city reflected
what couriers endure
her love occurs to me
without slumber
who has recourse to the pasture?
will she love me when i have recourse?
will she course through a city
and wc emerge/

and now we seem to be
coursing on luxury
clear and coursing and pretty
on the earth
coursing to sigh or to cover
coursing earth even emerging from bitter
ness and shivering
over the course of safe distancing
nuanced minutely and fucking
the coarse of such
coercive (course of) tenderness

of confidence and nostalgia

i circled your confidence
in the firs a confidence of birds
no posture was poetry's confidence
who was confident in their own administration of touch?
whose poetry disappeared into circling text like prey?
i touched your confident palm
of fondness i knew not
the confidence in my hand was a situation
of touch or nostalgia
along nostalgia, fondness' confidence
lyrics echo in the paved courtyard where firs host
confidences of birds
what flew this way and that in the text, slouched,
stretched? nostalgia
is glacial run-off
warm of course
from confident stanzas

of n

not folded in my suitcase
between insistence and displacement
in the fragile design of this
an antecedent trembles
now a graph of coursing blue
and the spectra of nouns
and this expressing
a sky

what suits me is this
in the shade of abstraction
we spread our blanket and lay back
serifs tickling our ears and scalp

our necks
although figuratively serious
edging away from the given nexus

our bodies entangled in the words
bed throws and hollows
solid arm askew this poem
as though solidity trembles

of naturally

of the state all humans naturally desire knowledge
now you spea
unless demystified, we pit
fear of bodies, which he believed i
called belief because milk i
a national affectation the
the subjection of eac
now you spea
their country and obe
dialecticians don't mea
we said devil
because they were pleased by the
husk of a word ho
cracking i

leaving the offices abandoned that were their fathers

Dear Son, the affectio
is like the win

you have that which would please most human
obedience that h
and blood, too, tha

adopt
due their ruler

(know this is the state)
but with pleasure
believed in good people

it cracks
the relief of "marriage"
the shadow follows not the cracking but the body

due your father
consumed by windmills

you'll see him under the surface of your old age

gave his lover
conducts time

OF CONTAINMENT
for the office of soft architecture, november 2006

We revel in the diffuse mists of a fountain as though we could forget containment and the clammy edges of ourselves. In increments, night descends, our reflections vanishing from the water's surface; and then may we withhold the trope of irony, close our eyelids to it like two splashes of cold ink.

This fountain is self-contained. Its surface seems smooth like that of an organ. Importunate minutiae flail outwards, are mist, impotent whims of containment. We wipe its ovoid surface the way we would an infant's closed fist. Its totality implicates us; we wipe it even though it is all water.

In Parc Lafontaine, a homeless girl steps out of the shadows to sell us chocolate. In the gridded and civic chocolate of holidays, too sweet, too sweet, we taste our attributes. Enchanting, cheeky. Reminiscent of our dissolute youth. Biting into chemicals, we clench our jaws. Then, as though this ch would dry our shivering skin, a handcloth, we rub ourselves with it, even quarrel over it.

Although now the fountain cools us, it does not allay our thirst for knowledge. Here is a tall and slender plume of water. Domestic memories are danced out by the water. With luck a girl is privileged by the wind, transgressing the dome suggested by the pool's circumference.

Some memories outgrow their inhabitance.

This fountain stands in a solitary stretch of paving at the top of Beaubien park. We take to the Outremont curb in a Durrellesque fantasy of imperialism and occupation, following the curve of the curb to the cure of the curfew, when dusk will turn us in to our bath salts and face creams, into domestic forgetfulness.

Although civic fountains now outdo both the domestic and garden fountain in popularity, domestic fountains were once popular with the rich. Among domestic fountains is one of a most luscious and inebriating sort: the table fountain, set up on banquet tables to amuse guests. Albrecht Durer's Design for a Gothic Table Fountain shows red spouts from which wine would eddy, producing desirable lovers where equivalent pools had been. Up on the dry land, under the twisting vines, bucolic and lively figures tend sheep and dance with abandon. We record this scenographic clutter with love's fingers.

Then it is that the banquet moves to the bedroom, where we are eroticized. Anyone choosing to enjoin this frivolous and equivocal diversion will be pleased to note the table fountain in the shape of a hyperbolic foam-flower, its focused slope of wine, gravity's resistance, laughter bubbling and pooling at the bottom. We enter the bedroom, focusing down hope, as though enacting an allegory. We unhook our fine frocks, clumsily getting caught in the gauze, and we peer through our gauze contentiously. In the maudlin and soft-stockinged porn shots in the window display, we find that the bedroom is a facade. If nothing else, surely the frontal view of nude mothers in fountains, streaming milk from their breasts, would point us to the myth of inhabitance. The bedroom is none other than a frontage itself; an interior domestic is all ghostliness. We are nostalgic for it as for a nostalgic poetic.

OF THE MIDDLE

of the middle

Our language with no body, nor less breath running.
Our language less in motion than motion.
Our tongues between properties, dividing
nipples, the centrelanguage, heartbeat.
By the middle of September I had no body,
I was centrelanguage dividing the missing heartbeat,
my heartbeat, from the present.
By the middle of September I had no property, no body.
By the middle.

I bled language until I had no body.
Between our properties dividing turnips
from snow in the cold bare
vicinity of our language.
By the middle of winter
our story was less motion, language bled from me.
By the middle, I was a missing person
dividing months from the human
language with no body
honeycombs
frozen
honed
shhhh
but
I cannot breathe nor run with this less language.

I bled language until I had no body.
Bled between turnips and snow
Bled the cold bare language.
By the middle
Our story was less
Language had bled from me
So our story was less.

What if a final s were to elide the text?
Slipping into non-being, slipping off the
very end. If it were fragile. As it fell to the
pavement, a glass s cracking.

In time, seedlings begin to grow around
the shards of this s. One of them, a solid
tree, will break through the s' fragmented
curve, transform it into topsoil.

The s had a story, but she was lost in time.
The elision of time. Splinters the very
touch. This idea of authenticity drawn
from the writer like a splinter/ this idea of
authenticity splintered for the writer/ this
idea of the writer/ this idea of convected
heat/ of fingers/ of her mechanistic body/
of ideas splintered and wedged in her body

The cycle of elision and broken ease,
accepted and rejected sensuality. If I were
to write a whole sentence, would it be to
redeem?

When we bring glass s's outside and dare
them to break. When we undo ease,
disillusion.

of love

I mistook love for an ending.
An ending love for a mistake.

                There is no love without mistakes.

I mistook a tree for love. An ending.

You wrapped us up in love and mistakes.

I was already over. Time mistook me.
Wrapped in leaves/gales.

Time over us. I
mistook no love
for a mistake.

Despite you.

An ending is love
of an ending

There is no I.

You are us.
Wrapped up in a mistake.

An ending loves an ending.
Not your mistake.
Just love already over.

of "the"/ the masculine/ the feminine

Divide the lines into two groups.
Those containing the masculine article
and those containing the feminine.
Some lines belong to both groups.

In a different arrangement, these lines form
a refrain on the stanza's fringes.
          Wind blows up the library stairs.

We take refuge in the books whose languages
have yet to break us.

Breaking the will is the/a reflex of our
language (that has no will).

Handwriting recollects
the body, the broken body.

of between

between the precious and the radical
between the strategic and the tragic
radiant and strained
fountain is a folding fan of water.
the pressure of errant streams
massages precious togetherness open.
from the fissure clear water issues
as though from a purse
between clasps of discourses
and their embroidered surfaces

between the institutions of pairs

the middle is a guess of worn surfaces
between the privilege of two
between the two of conformity
or the two of caution

if vanity is between us
as much as
we have yet to break

between the surfaces of singing
and the surfaces of speaking
entre tes braz trestoute nue

of the still middle

still in the what happens middle of never

still in the what middle happens of never

still in the middle what happens of never

still in the middle what of happens never

still in the middle of what happens never

still in the middle of what never happens

in still the middle of what never happens

in the still middle of what never happens

in the still of middle what never happens

in the of still middle what never happens

in of the still middle what never happens

of in the still middle what never happens

BARRETTE

To barrette one's hair is to relinquish authority over the external world while garnishing the internal: example of unruly hair as metaphor for second-guessing oneself. The coterminous metonymic trajectory – barrette belonging to "woman" – suggesting an essentialist conclusion. But what is a barrette? It is not "the woman's" fingers, which could hold her hair only while restricting the movements of her body in general. Perhaps the barrette is the ungendered fingers of a second body. Perhaps a claw, a clasp, a clip, a cunt. The beasts of "their" are clenched in an epidemic of authority. They argue for the holding fingers rather than the pen, they argue for the fingers gliding across the keys. (Above all, they know this to be an argument for themselves.) Their arguments mimic war as though victory or defeat were inevitable. But what if implements did not suggest subjects – if "their" implements did not suggest "them"; if "their barrettes" were neither the hands of another in servitude nor the hands of another oppressing "them"?

It is not easy to maintain the position of a barrette. If it is heavy with ornamentation it slides down. It resembles a philosophical proof loaded with metaphor. If the hair is thin, the barrette's grip slackens, becomes insecure. The hair behind the ear sticks out, is improper, and the nape of the neck obscured by lies. If the tongue is a liar, and the inane hairs sticking to it. Now the hairstyle is potentially ruined. Temporary muteness ensues, as they pull hairs from their tongues.

Maintaining one's position and maintaining one's positioning are two very different exercises in the world of argumentation. In the world as argument, arguably. In the world one's position is arguably negligent of one's positioning in that world. This is the argument we hold against those who hold or gain power; this is our argument. How one positions oneself in relation to oppressive phenomena must be valuable in and of itself, and yet the value placed on one's position in an argument generally comes to supersede the value of one's positioning. Why is that?

(the barrette slides down
the commodity loses its aura
potential disaster – desirable potency)

Before the prospect of bottomless human existence, we relinquished authority over any route to the internal. Example of unruly human assessment: a coterminous them. To carouse is to unbridge "belonging" and "woman" in each illusion and in consequent instances of disillusion, to retrace love. We argued over whether we should bridge or unbridge se-x-es. Many simply could not accept the barrette binary. We wondered, what is the function of a barrette, now? Was it once different? What of its childhood dreams and debts which could hold her hair only. What of love as the ultimate avènement of her body in general. The adventurous termingendered fingers of a second unbridging the human. Again, these beasts of endemic authority. They argue for us, an ornament in the hair. They argue for the s. They know this to es. They argue the es and the s of historical rhetoric, following the same route to the internal. But what if their hems (n.b. Lost referent. We noted that whether we hemmed with an s or an es, a concealed internal was inevitable).

n.b. In prospect of bottomless human existence, the lost referent would be considered a relinquished authority only if there had ever been some authority to relinquish. Is an implement defined as what can be used by a subject? Does metonymy refer to the whole via the part or the subject via the implement? Whence the implement as part of a whole?

In the world without bars, the city is still a set of coded habits: walk to the same store for cheese, milk, pears and bread, in the same shadows of buildings, blurred in the habit of walking them. To carouse is to unbrick the side of a house built by one's ancestors, and to see each brick clearly, its lines, texture of its familial dreams and debts. Theirs was always the dream of love as the ultimate adventure. The debts are ultimately unpaid, the adventure terminates in the repeated act of unbricking the house. Again and again and all this for love.

They are ornaments in the hair of Love.

In the unbarred world, language negotiates intimacy the way water negotiates the fountain. Intimacy is distorted by language but not obscured. It is worn by the current of language, it is transformed. When we go against the current of language, we step on the stones of intimacy. We step into the current. We step onto more deeply submerged stones. We step into the current.

Enduring intimacy comes undone. The hardness of stone is undone: metal pebble lintel steel stone bronze brick barrette rock cubic-arch hard pebble pillar sculpture plaisance pretty steel temple language flowing over this pitted hard sculpture. Enduring intimacy comes undone in this nothing-before-language (this not even Love).

We are ornaments slipping down the hair of Love

Mistakenly placed and descending the hair of Love

OF POTENTIAL

of emergency exits

Stepping aside to allow others to pass in a gallery, she finds herself in a darkened corner, between a fire escape and oneirism, this small press of wall a dreamy side show over which is cast her most precious, cautionary domestic memories. The red SORTIE sign is a source of superstition, encoded and rehearsed. Self-effacement characterizes her sidestep in as much as ceding characterizes her sense of self. Constant yielding of belief prepares one for such sidestepping. So, the emergency exit is never used, but it is impossible to hang art over it.

Rituals of necessity are seen to redeem building codes. In a public space, where an empty corner takes on a cavernous quality, the domestic might be conjured, under the sign of caution and fire, a public site for transformation.

of potentiality

If Reason were to abandon symmetry, become the water falling around her head. Hide her face in an extended form of logic, a gutter. Falling away, the self-same water exhorts its disappearance. What falls away is a narrative's essential prologue.

She would be composed of asymmetrical sentences that fall about her in infinitely layered patterns. The potential in these layers is drawn from intuition like a curtain. This curtain once divided the space between deduction and intuition. Drawn potential may be a light and airy fabric or a heavy velvet. Some prefer deep rose or red curtains.

A curtain drawn beside grey days. Evening. Long winters of potentiality. À côté de. Blue light of water and snow. For a moment she is motionless. Plumes in her hat waver in a gentle wind. The fountain's course is undisturbed.

of conditions

The allegory described a physical world in which material was a language unbounded by notions of gravity. I wanted to spread dissent, yet I wrote across the back of the countryside from the vantage of a city. Though I resisted gravity, I found myself in a condition of absolute torpor and abjection, akin to immersed, swirling sand.

I wanted to was a language unbounded by reality. I wanted to be real, I found. I wrote on the back of what I found from my vantage point. If the nation had emerged beside the notion of gravity, I wanted a physical world. I wanted to be immersed in the nation's gravity. I wanted to determine whether repairing from gravity was what I sought from language or whether immersing in gravity was what I sought from language. I found each instance of wanting to be a condition newly unbounded. I despaired and I repaired. I exalted wanting and yet could no longer claim to know that state, the conditions for wanting having come unlaced.

How can I tell you what I know?

How could I claim to have ever told you?

(descending velocity at which the speed of our body

speed of a fountain, blurred, and the speed

our body disappeared in the fountain becoming

a second body and therewith all of) Which was a second body where

between the covers of two languages seven allegorized sins lined a

garden wall and wary of enacting exteriorized interpretations of a

function cut short of inhabiting a language any language as though

it were not the lover's body but one's own, [her] body continued [its

unsettled] fountaining display of inhabitance without acknowledging

the temporal aspect of its existence embodying g(end)er without

continuance an embodiment of discontinuous temporality stopped

short at the vellum sheet corner which would fade to the point where

only f's were visible centuries later, their enduring downstrokes

66

of potential

of the potential in a random root
becoming visible. an abyss is potential
becoming image. film's shudder
in the cinema where potential viewers
brush their knees against each other. a dry
fountain, heard rush, fabric rustling
into potential touch. how to speak of poetry?
rush of vowels from the fountain of
becoming entrance.
mischievous decisions made for potential renewal.
a melancholic poet's
muse? going blind for the potential of sight?
not an unsatisfied-wanting-more but
moving at the potential speed of water
through an evaporating world

of disappearance

I disappeared
into discontinuous contact
between water and bone
into the fountain
its seemingly perpetual movement
drawn restless I an abyss

transversion (a potentiality already actualized and therefore impotent)

I disappeared into discontinuous contact between water and bone. Into the fountain, its seemingly perpetual movement. Into the place of discontinuous contact where *the question of movement became associated with the subject's entrance into the image, with rites of passage.* In this ritual place where the figure, I, becomes the fountain, a visible transformation.

Potentiality makes a visible abyss in the fountain.

> as restless as water
> welcome I into the
> would disappear

APPENDICES A, B AND C

GLOSS

This book was conceived of as an allegorical mall with a central fountain and concordance corridors leading away from it in several directions. Amid mass-produced goods and consumers, perched on the brim of the central fountain, sits the poet, otherwise known as Poverty, dipping her hand into the water to retrieve coins. Over the loudspeakers play the voices of a slowed-tempo chorus of literary critics. The entire scene is in black and white except for the green basin of the fountain and the green money exchanging hands across counters. The sculptural feature of the fountain is a gorgeous representation of Narcissus, whose face is turned down toward the water. Directly above the fountain, there is a round opening in the ceiling with the inscription "Our Pink Heaven" in a ring around its edge. The sky above is grey. (Note the mall must be closed when the sky is blue and when it is raining).

The allegory appears on the surface to be a closed system. Corridors terminate in banality and inconclusiveness. (Plans for a mirror corridor were finally omitted, its features dispersed to other parts of the mall). Truth is the face of reflection, a most expensive faiblesse in this world of rapid exchange; Beauty encodes the towardness of grey thickening, is aloof and unpredictable as weather.

In contrast to the busyness of the mall, on the opposite side of the street there are two billboards showing medieval illuminations.

Behind these panels, a flat, grassy landscape stretches to the horizon. On the first panel, in the foreground of a similarly flat landscape, the Dreamer is seen asleep on a grey stone slab, which curls underneath him like a single, open quotation mark. This is the dreamer who once narrated the *Roman de la Rose* in his sleep. Is he a somnambulist? For in the next panel, he is seen washing his hands in a fountain. His hair is blue, and blue is the water.

Songes et mensonges, dreams and lies. The vast expanse of grassy openness and blue sky behind the panels intoxicates, revives an indefatigable dream of freedom.

The poet was hesitant to encroach on allegory from a modernist point of view. She thought she would rather encounter it as she does the city, by understanding it as a series of quartiers and rues, or even as the Hôtel dieu, with its tidy, finite corridors and impermanent inhabitants. She saw there was nothing permanent or integral about the allegory. Whereas,

A system of signification is a dose of moral parity.
A system of signification constructs levels for enamoured cruelty.
A system of signification dismisses manifoldly.

The system of signification manifestoed and plotted against was not as polished as she would appear many years later (after her lexicon fell). Hence the revolution, during which allegory's terms were to be freed, tattooed on the stony bust of the lute player.

GLOSS

INVISIBLE CHORUS OF LITERARY CRITICISM (EXTREMELY SLOWLY): A singular body, when considered the terminus of any amorous relationship, is both defined and undermined by love. Body and term emerge on the outer limits of love and meaning respectively. Allegorical, the Terminus is a potential body, an anthropomorphous third party marking a boundary, delineating bodies in love. The Terminus is the vanishing point of the meaning of love. The term love, and in fact the entire lyrical provenance of love, beckons at the limits of allegory, where poets would carry all their material.

GLOSS

POET: How hard is the heart that loves not in May
Moult a dur cuer qui en mai n'aime

APPENDIX B

details from the omitted mirror corridor

for the last time, hanging her legs off the bed

comfortably mirrored pursuit

through smoke the natural pursues comfort relentlessly

ontology of mirrors or the teasing real

is there reason to apprehend

mirrors in the field of mourning

her voice's mirror

draws her under

makes the mirrored surface into a garment

and the warm sunlight on her thighs

dons it and becomes unseen

only in grief were the mirrors absent

this one through smoke became

and

in grief the sensation of mirrors became

and

in grief the   absent

in grief

(chorus) a baleful sheen of lack undulates
beneath our mirrored desire for the future
and beneath that, the language of our past

APPENDIX C

of love and argument (remix)

25   how i love words
90   of the fountain through love
171   in whose night and day were types of grain argued
183   i read this worst love is a no
217   if our love has been outdistanced
242   what uncovered loves?
247   monogamous love are you in pain?
248   over love runs the tail of mutton
276   her love occurs to me
279   will she love me when I have recourse?
402   scenographic clutter with love's fingers
481   i mistook love for an ending
482   an ending love for a mistake
483   there is no love without mistakes
484   i mistook a tree for love. an ending.
485   you wrapped us up in love and mistakes.
489   mistook no love
492   an ending is love
497   an ending loves an ending
499   just love already over
523   they argue for the holding
524   they know this to be an argument for
527   their arguments mimic war
543   one's position is arguably negligent
544   the argument we hold

545   against those who hold or gain power; this is our argument
549   one's position in an argument
561   consequent instances of disillusionment, to retrace love
562   we argued over
563   what of love as the ultimate avènement
568   they argue the es and s
573   always the dream of love as the ultimate
576   and again and all this for love
577   they are ornaments in the hair of Love
590   this nothing-before-languages (this not even Love)
591   they are ornaments slipping down the hair of Love
592   mistakenly placed and descending the hair of Love

542   in the world as argument, arguably
562   we argue over
523   authority. They argue for the holding
576   and again and all this for love
568   they argue the es and s
242   what uncovered loves?

Acknowledgements

Thanks to Oana Avasilichioaei, Brenda Cockfield, Jay MillAr, Erín Moure, the Office for Soft Architecture, and Alisha Piercy. Thanks to Daniel Canty for translating Sleep Water into French and allowing me to remix his translated lines on page 23.

Many texts and artworks informed this book, including Jospeh R. Danos' *A concordance to the Roman de la Rose of Guillaume de Lorris*, Giorgio Agamben's *Stanza: Word and Phantasm*, translated by Ronald L. Martinez, the Bourdillon collection of *Roman de la Rose* manuscripts at the National Library of Wales, Aberystwyth, Lisa Robertson's *Occasional Work and Seven Walks from the Office for Soft Architecture*, and Suzanne Dery's show of ink drawings at the Centre Culturel de Frontenac in 2006, *fontaine*. The italicized line on page 69 is from *Aby Warburg and the image in motion*, by Philippe-Alain Michaud, translated by Sophie Hawkes. The quote from Walter Benjamin's *Arcades Project* is from the translation by Howard Eiland and Kevin McLaughlin.

Some of these texts have previously appeared in: *The Capilano Review, Dandelion, Jacket, Matrix, Poetry Wales* and in the collection *Translating Translating Montréal* (2007). Thanks to the editors.

About the Author

Angela Carr is the author of *Ropewalk* (2006).
She lives and works in Montréal.

COLOPHON

Manufactured in an edition of 500 copies in the summer
of 2009 | Distributed in Canada by the Literary Press
Group WWW.LPG.CA | Distributed in the United States
by Small Press Distribution WWW.SPDBOOKS.ORG |
Shop on-line at WWW.BOOKTHUG.CA

BOOK
PRODUCTION
WAR ECONOMY
STANDARD

Type + design by Jay MillAr
Edited for the press by Oana Avasilichioaei